The Old Works

Whittney Jones

The Heartland Review Press/Elizabethtown, KY

Copyright©2019 Whittney Jones

All rights reserved

This book may not be reproduced, in whole or in part, including illustrations, in any form (beyond that copying permitted by Section 107 and 108 of the Us Copyright Law and except by reviewers for the public press), without written permission from the publisher.

First Edition

Printed in the USA

ISBN 978-0-9996868-7-4

$8.00

To view The Heartland Review Press full
catalog of books visit www.theheartlandreview.com

Table of Contents

Coal	3-4
The First Year of Marriage	5
The Punch Line	6
Blast Zone	7
Willow Lake Mine	8
The Dollar Value of Fingers	9
The Old Works	10
I'm in St. Louis to Find You	11-12
Mine	13-14
Man of Coal	15-16
Wildcat Hills	17-18
Black Lung Screening	19
The Price of Coal	20-21
The Underground	22
Bloodlines	23
Camel Rock–Shawnee National Forest	24
Will Scarlet Mine	25-26

The Old Works

*For Adam,
and, to Indy: everything.*

Coal

To explain coal when you've never
seen it, except as the black liner drawn

under your husband's eyes or the grit
that gathers in the washing

machine and stains everything
after it. It's the black rock surfacing

as pock marks in the folds
of my favorite shirt, in the toes

of socks, tinging all of the bright
colors dim, even the reflector

tape banding the knees
of his pants has gone

dull with gunk. To explain
coal when you've never felt

it, except in the hours among
two and four, when he was due

home at one, and you can recall
how long they went before calling

when the roof fell on his brother.
It sounds like the silence

in between the beats
of your pulse, the soft,

sad whine of our daughter dreaming
of things that scare her. To explain

coal when you've never breathed
it in— it smells like the inside

of his dirty lunch box, like all
the Tupperware I've trashed

when it wouldn't come
clean. It's a life of mine

clothes in plastic Wal-Mart
sacks stacked next to the door

and empty cups and fast
food bags in the car

when he didn't get his turn
for lunch. Coal is the sick, secret

feeling you get in the bottom
of your gut when you consider

the weight of money over
black lung, over an early

grave, and you, alone, in this
world for what will come

to pennies. Coal feels like
letting the Ohio current

carry your water-logged body home.

The First Year of Marriage

We walk the shoreline
of the Ohio not touching
so nothing keeps
winter from numbing
our fingers. I stop
to watch the dead things
float by—a hollowed
log bobbing the current,
the pale glisten of a fish
belly, an accompanying stink.
The crests push to comb
the edges for more debris,
lapping at the toes
of our shoes, where they sink
in mud and squelch when we lift
them up. You tell me
we've been here too long
and move on. Birds call
to one another, scavenge
what they can from the shallows.
Empty mussel shells lie
shine-down, half-buried to hide
the broken parts—their insides,
pearl white, pretty, and barren.

The Punch Line

after Kim Addonizio's, "Ha"

A man walks into a bar,
but this is not a joke. I'm with him,

drunk, and we've come so he can buy
me another, maybe to kiss me

or get me to bed. I'm in love,
concentrating hard on what

he's saying, so I don't say it
first, but he doesn't say it either.

Marriage is a three ring
circus: engagement ring,
wedding ring, suffering.

He laughs and next asks
if I've heard the one about

the priest who drinks his Guinness
with the hand that holds

his rosary. When we leave,
it's snowing, and we're the two

losers on the corner asking
why our affair was doomed to be

short-lived. Not that either of us
knows we're in it, even then.

Blast Zone

They coat the coal with rock
dust to keep it from igniting

under the sun. The gob
pile is a long, black mountain

range behind the cemetery where we bury
the men who never made it above

the poverty line. And look
at all the wildlife

we've killed for heat
though the birds still would have

abandoned their young
just from our touch. I crush

the blue eggs, digging my fingers
into my palm, to birth

the yolk, saved, as the Earth separates
by dynamite and we pollute the sky

with our sad demands
and the land resettles again

in lonely muted colors, the stomach
gutted, our insides torn loose.

Willow Lake Mine

> *Located in Equality, IL, the mine closed after the accidental death of a miner in 2012.*

I know the EMT
who attended him, pressed
an empty chest and counted

after they found him pinned by the continuous
miner's hooked teeth. His foot in the red
zone. His fingers not quite working

the controls still in his grip. Waiting
long minutes for someone to realize
he was an insect caught in a shadowbox.

I know the EMT who came home
and showered and showered and slept
poorly. Who started folding overalls

into boxes. Halved and halved. Lunch
box left on the linoleum, a silhouette
of coal dust outlining where it dropped—

a chalk dust tracing of a body
for MSHA to examine and declare:
death, closure, tragedy, regulations.

I know the EMT who held the tattoo
canary on his bicep, who willed
breath into his burdened lungs, who cried

for him, who knew the caged bird
on the boy's arm opened to an illustrated
coal mine on the other side, and the creature,

pinned, suffocates.

The Dollar Value of Fingers

A pinky taken in the mines is worth
ten thousand dollars. A forefinger goes

for five times more. You always wanted
to get out of here, this small town.

The only thing for an unschooled boy
like you to do is dig deep

for coal. The same that blackens
your snot and the underside

of your fingernails, that traces
the hard, calloused lines of your palms

and streaks me with its war paint
when you run your hands over

my stomach, your forefinger tracing
symbols I can't read, and I try

to remember the room I used to have
in me for this, when all that mattered

was that we could hold onto each other.
Now, the want of fifty thousand

dollars, how maybe it could
save us.

The Old Works

I imagine it as a cave filled
with the broken things—ancient
mantrips, snapped joy sticks, scraps

of belts, the odd riddling of coal
rocks that crumble when you pick
them up, chalking your fingertips.

Flagged with yellow tape
like a crime scene, examined
on and off again—for bad bolts, flexing

tops, high gas readings—before
it's filled up. They've used it
all and gone on. Forgotten

until the blacktops start to sink,
settle, and break apart. They've closed
down Harco, trying to make it

a road again. People remember you're down
there and complain about their foundation,
the detours, the road home, and how, no matter

how many times it's paved, it goes
with the giving dirt, after everything
beneath has been taken away.

I'm in St. Louis to Find You

The rise of your pants
is the arch of St Louis.
Your belt buckle, the gateway

to city lights, a life fast-paced
and hungry beneath our feet.
Your kisses are the windows—

press to see the world
outside. My breath fogs
the glass where I can draw

shapes like hearts,
our initials over a view
of the river. Hold my hand

when the bend dances in a gust
of wind. I can't tell if I'm moving,
or if it's you, or if the ground

has become so unsteady
that everything's moving now.
I don't know what to liken

to the sex we haven't had.
Maybe it's the souvenir shop
beneath us, where we find a mug

or book to take home and shelve.
My hands unbuttoning your shirt,
yours on my hips, your voice on

my lips saying you didn't think
it'd be so hard to stop. Don't
shelve me. Make me that postcard

memory, that tram ride
you remember when you look back,
holding your breath to peak

at the top when the elevator
stops and we are six hundred feet
above rational thought.

There's barely room to move, pressed
together as we look out across
the dark Mississippi. The heat

of your body, the jump
of your pulse. I want to be
that spectacular trip, your favorite

thrill: standing at the top of the arch
looking down, dizzy in the knees,
your gut in your throat, your heart

in your head—until the next
group comes, and we're ushered
out to the end.

Mine

It's the night Robbie made the joke
then started ralphing before
the punch line. You had to help him up
into the cab of his truck, where he slumped
and giggled against the dash.

The night Porky's wife wouldn't stop
talking to me through the Port-o-Potty's
plastic and Benny pissed his pants drunk
but didn't know, still trying to hand out
barbecue after tossing back that whole bottle
of bourbon the wives had been using to take

shots while their husbands sloshed
beer down their fronts and ribbed
whoever had cut a cable last shift
or shit too close to the only clear path
through the Return. That bastard.

You know, when J.D. moped
all night over that crazy Chicago girl
with the drawn-on eyebrows whose nipple
I had accidentally seen after a night
of gambling and you pretended
to be plastered so we could leave.

That pole barn party—
when we took the gravel roads
in my Pontiac, idling just beyond
the Warning: Blast Zone signs outside
of Wildcat, where Peabody had bought
out the houses lining the cracked
blacktop with the weeds growing
through the splits.

It was all natural light in the back
seat for the cramped, awkward sex
over the heads of who knew how many
red hats working the midnight shift,
just discovering how to use their hands.

It was that night we drove home
with the windows down, darkness only
settling in when we turned out the lights
in bed, your leg hooking mine, the same
way you label what's yours underground, learning
all at once someone else could take it.

Man of Coal

You must be there, where the road
sinks, where the sign reads bump, uneven
pavement, where the earth has sunk
down over your head.

I feel her move like that, our baby—
sudden, shifting, never
answering the press of my hand.
Is that how the world moves
for you?

I think I hear your voice
there, through the concrete's
cracks, echoing in the bowls
of potholes, asking
what else is there here?

There were mountains, now
moved to plains. Brown, turned
soil as far as we can see, no
trees, every curled root pulled
free. I've seen the machine.

You bring the coal home
to me in your clothes, the creases
of your skin. I dream we press it
into diamonds between us
and live off the sum

never to be paid back
with bones or blood or the color
of your lungs, their capacity to fill
up, to breathe my name before
sleep when we link hands beneath

the pillows, to tell me of your dreams
outside of the underground, and I ache
to write them into the real, the now.
I'll write the forest back
to life, just ask me.

Wildcat Hills

There's a forest
fossilized underground.

I dream of them—each
outlined skeleton,

bones

crushed into the dark
shadows that shape

them. They have
faces,

even the trees. You can
see whole limbs,

each leaf

a perfect, pointed
oval.

They hang overhead, as if to shade

you from a sun neither
of you can remember

seeing.

Their voices sound like a moaning
wind, the kind

that makes you feel more hollow
than cold. The most common

fossil is the snail,
but just the spiral of the shell

survived

the process of sinking
into sediment, of standing

under pressure. None
are preserved

now. There are still millions
of live snails to take each

entombed

snail's place. A machine carves
them loose, crumbles

their shadow skeletons
into dust. It's in

your lungs.

Everyone says that breathing
will come less easy

over time. I spend
long hours in the evening, rocking

our daughter to sleep, thinking

of how I might dig you up,
how to save you from

the rock and the mud
as it's settling.

Black Lung Screening

He has the hack
already, the gravel
cough. He swallows
half the earth he's dug
up. He's still coated

in rock
at the hospital,
the night a ram car
almost crushes
him, and shakes,
like he can't stand

up. All this time waiting
for the test results,
as if the worst
could be how much
of his lungs
is dirt and dark grit.

The Price of Coal

Flood season brings drought to the mouth
of our home. We started pulverizing

our own green beans and sweet potatoes
in the spring for our daughter, as familiar

with the price of formula as jarred
vegetables after last year and the jaundice

without the breast milk I couldn't produce,
and you without work

so long as the coal can't float
to the power plants. The hunger

for warmth depleted by clean
energy. The wind devastates us

until the call comes for more. Contracts
signed for a few fleeting years until

we have to decide again whether we move
or stay in a small town in Illinois, reverting

to the ghosts and abandoned factories
that own it. You and I are this drift

mine, cut into the side of a hill
slowly giving way, bargaining

our lives on recoverable reserves
that kiss us, fickle, on the mouth.

Twenty-seven million tons don't matter
without demand. Blame Obama, blame

strict reform, blame Prometheus, who damned
us all with fire. Blame each other

for what we can't provide. Let the water
recede before we drift apart. How wide

the Ohio seems from this side
to Kentucky. From this end

to the money.

The Underground

She births them, same as any, from her hips,
at shift-end, soot-thick and near unrecognizable,
already greedy to have them again, to carve their marks
against her insides, to keep forever, pinned to shaved sediment
inside the red zone, where the tail of the machine swings,
clutching them to her breast. She would fossilize
them, keep their bones to rub against.

She would remind them of Woman, almighty,
in the otherwise sexless face of the dark and dank
and deep. She tried to take you with a ram car.

Remember, before all of this, when coal
was just a rock pile outlining country roads?

Bloodlines

They won't let him work

with his brother

obliterate

an entire bloodline

should it come down

we have

a daughter

to compensate

the long hours

I'm alone

her arms his

embracing my neck

to say it's okay

we did

what we had

to live.

Camel Rock – Shawnee National Forest

The hills closer to home are all
pitch black. I ask you how they'll reclaim
something like that—the discarded shale
and sandstone. You call it gob,
what Peabody doesn't want.

They'll make it a mountain
and cover it in dirt
so by the time your kids
are old enough to remember,
they won't.

Not like here, where only the wind could
smooth the formations the water cut
from rock. We sun ourselves
on the camel's hump and never brave
the jump to the head, watching others
toe the edge, indifferent to the risk.

This is a forest that coal
can't touch. This is a preserve
for refugees like us.

Will Scarlet Mine

> "Abandoned strip mining sites in the southeast corner of Williamson County that have been identified by the Illinois Department of Natural Resources as some of the most toxic spots in the Midwest are causing concern for county officials."
> *--The Southern Illinoisan*

I'll redress you as the success
grand tales have made us

from red mud. We sculpt
the sludge into trees and mold

birds into their branches. I dig
a lake with my finger, so clear

the fish won't swim there. The heron
won't land, even in the shallows. I blend

the red beneath my nails into the grass, etch
deer and whatever else might live here.

Houses? People loved in these skeletal
remains, in these boards clinging

by tooth of rusty nail. Names unravel
with the curling wallpaper, exposing initials

carved into wood, people carved
into the detail. The gate

is for looks. I push it from its hinges,
and it falls loose, kicking up dust

in the gravel. We roll in the thick
grass and find fragments of Mason jars

made into the dirt, scraping
the beaded-sweat of our backs, and wonder

at what was preserved
for winter, here in the thick

of the long-gone corn fields, naked
cobs half-buried in the ruts. You learn

to like it here, in the papier-mâché
trees. No one else comes down

this road to enjoy the silence, the vast
expanse of stars. We hold

hands and reclaim each other
in the breaths we share

with our lips pressed together.
Exhale. I'll draw the black

from your lungs.

Acknowledgments

Eternal gratitude to the readers and editors who selected these poems for publication in the following journals: "The Punch Line" in *Jet Fuel Review*; "The Dollar Value of Fingers" in *Ninth Letter*; "Man of Coal" in *Switchback*; "Coal" in *The Heartland Review*; "I'm in St. Louis to Find You" and "The First Year of Marriage" in *Alligator Juniper*; "Will Scarlet Mine" and "Wildcat Hills" in *Third Coast*; "Willow Lake Mine" in *The Crab Orchard Review*. Special thanks to the judges of The Illinois Emerging Writers Competition for selecting "The Dollar Value of Fingers" and "The Price of Coal" for the Gwendolyn Brooks Poetry Award in 2014 and 2016 respectively.

About the author:

Whittney Jones grew up in southern Illinois, and her writing considers life in her small hometown. Focusing primarily on how coal, the last of, if not the only, remaining profitable careers in an area on the wrong side of the poverty line, shapes the life of her family, Jones attempts to rationalize sticking around and making it work, while the rest of the world works to leave fossil fuels behind. Jones is winner of the 2014 Gwendolyn Brooks Poetry Prize in The Illinois Emerging Writers Competition and a finalist in the 2017 and 2019 International Literary Awards Rita Dove Poetry Prize. Her poems have been published in such literary magazines as *The Crab Orchard Review*, *Ninth Letter*, *Zone 3*, *the minnesota review*, and *Alligator Juniper*.

www.ingramcontent.com/pod-product-compliance
Lightning Source LLC
Chambersburg PA
CBHW070442010526
44118CB00014B/2165